DOING APOLOGETICS

ELGIN HUSHBECK

Topical Line Drives
Volume 36

Energion Publications
Gonzalez, Florida
2019

Cover Design: Henry E. Neufeld

ISBN: 978-1-63199-696-2

Energion Publications
PO Box 841
Gonzalez, FL 32560

http://energion.com
pubs@energion.com

ACKNOWLEDGMENTS

Numerous people have influenced my opinions on how to do apologetics; more importantly, how not to do it. While this is a short book, it is based on my experience over several decades. I wish to thank everyone who played a role in shaping the views I express; those who supported me, and those who did not. I also greatly appreciate the extremely valuable editing and comments of Helen Wisniewski. And of course, I must thank my friend and editor Henry Neufeld for his efforts and support.

INTRODUCTION

Christian apologetics has its ups and downs. There are those who see it as a positive force defending the Christian faith against the attacks of critics. Still others see a far more negative force trying to argue people into the Kingdom of God, or even worse, arguing simply for argument's sake. Most of the time it is just ignored. As one who has a master's degree in Christian Apologetics, is the author of two books that hopefully fall into the positive-force category, (*Evidence for the Bible* and *Christianity and Secularism*) with a third one (*Faith and Reason*) on the way, and who has been doing this for several decades, I do consider myself to be a Christian apologist. Over this time, I have developed some thoughts on the proper role for apologetics and how I believe, one should do it.

First, I would agree there are some merits to criticism of apologetics. I would certainly agree that apologetics can be misused, done incorrectly or for the wrong reasons, though I would quickly point out the same is true of most things. Think of what damage a pastor or priest can do if they are not working as a true servant of God, yet that would hardly be a reason to give up on the role of pastor, rather it would be a reason to act correctly and for the right reasons.

I would also agree we should not try to argue people into the Kingdom of God, and I have consistently taught in my ministry this is not the role of apologetics. The reason is simple: it does not work, and if that is why someone uses apologetics, they are wasting their time.

Of course, this raises the question of why do apologetics? A simple one is we are commanded to do so in passages like 1 Peter 3:15-16,

> *Instead, exalt the Messiah as Lord in your lives. Always be prepared to give a defense to everyone who asks you to explain the hope you have. But do this gently and respectfully, keeping a clear conscience, so that those who speak evil of your good conduct in the Messiah will be ashamed of slandering you.*

The first part of this verse may be familiar to you. I would hope the second half would be equally familiar. Unfortunately, often the "gently and respectfully" part gets left off. It should not as it is key.

There are practical reasons for doing apologetics as well. True, no one is argued into the kingdom, but they can be helped to the foot of the cross. One of the ways I teach this is with the metaphor of a wall. We all like to build walls to keep God at a safe distance. Christians build these walls as well as non-Christians, but our focus here is on the non-believer who build walls of excuses so they can ignore God. The individual bricks making up these walls, i.e., beliefs and excuses on why they can ignore God, are many and varied:

- Religion, in general, is a destructive force that is little more than a tool of the powerful to enslave and oppress people.
- Religion is an irrational belief that has led to tremendous suffering and is behind most wars.
- Christianity is one of the greatest offenders, because of its vast power structures and influence.
- Christianity depends on a book written when there was no science but only superstition.

- The Bible cannot be trusted as it was edited and put together by church councils to retain their power base.
- The Bible cannot be trusted; it is full of contradictions and errors.
- The Bible has been disproven by science.

Or so the story goes. These are typical of the bricks that make up the walls keeping people from God. Now, these walls are built and reinforced by a popular culture growing increasingly hostile to people of faith, particularly Christians.

Of course, there are good answers to all of these, and the many other objections raised by critics. It is the role of apologetics to bring down those walls brick by brick till nothing is standing between the person and the cross. There is nothing to hide behind, and they must confront the message of redemption. At that point, the role of apologetics in evangelism ends. What happens next is between the person and the Holy Spirit.

While no can be argued into the kingdom, some have been brought to the foot of the cross, and thus apologetics does play an important role in their conversion. I know this to be the case, for I was one of those brought to the foot of the cross. I was an atheist who had built up a nice big comfortable wall consisting of a long list of reasons why I could safely ignore God. In fact, I was so comfortable behind my wall, I used it to take potshots at Christians. What about this, or what about that? Most of the time I was able to walk away, confident my wall had withstood the challenge as most Christians had no idea how to respond to the problems I raised and the questions I asked.

Occasionally, however, a Christian would point out a problem with one of my bricks. A flaw in the reasoning or evidence showing it was not quite the strong objection I had originally thought, and I would have to discard it. Still, that was not a big deal. After all, I had a lot of bricks in my wall, and discarding a few still left me with many others to hide behind. One by one over several years, a few Christians were able to answer these objections until they were no longer a barrier.

True, not everyone has such questions or objections, and thus for them, discussions on the reliability of the Bible, etc., would be irrelevant at best, possibly even counter-productive. This is why it is important to find out what it is that is keeping someone from the cross. Everyone has a wall, and every wall is unique. The first step is to discover what is keeping a person from God? Is it a question about the Bible? Is it a bad experience with a church or a Christian? Is it they have never really heard or considered Christianity? Before you can remove a wall, you must know the type of bricks. Apologetics cannot remove all bricks.

Now to be clear, I do not expect, or even believe, everyone would be or should be a trained apologist, ready with all the answers at their fingertips, any more than everyone would be or should be a pastor or a priest. Personally, one of the best answers someone can give to an objection from a critic is, "that is a good question, and I don't know. Let me find out and get back to you." I like this answer for many reasons. First, you don't need to have all the answers, only a resource where you can get them, if you do not know of one, then I recommend you start with your Pastor or Priest.

Secondly, it opens up a dialogue and begins building a relationship. I encourage people to be a safe place where those with questions can get answers; to be a person someone can ask a question without getting a full come-to-Jesus sermon. Perhaps it is because of my conversion experience, but I see conversion as more of a process than an event. A process taking a long time, and one in which, while there are many stages, there is no set order. Everyone is different, and this is why building a relationship is so key to evangelism. It is also why simply seeking to win the argument or defeating the opponent can be so counter-productive.

Furthermore, I want to say something in favor of intense debates; I have been in many, but intense does not mean disrespectful.

I caught the attention of my editor, many years ago, after he noticed me in an online forum engaging in some fairly intense debates, but remaining respectful, even when my opponents were not. While I engaged in such debates, there were times when I would wonder to myself, what is the point? These people never seem to change, and at times the argument seems to be going in circles.

Two things would keep me going.

1) I never told Christians I was debating whether or not they were right, when I was on the other side. Only afterward would I reflect on what they said, and I now believe the Holy Spirit used those arguments to work on my heart. In short, I do not need to see progress, for there to be progress.

2) Inevitably, at times when I was really discouraged, I would get an email from someone I had never heard of before or since, expressing thanks for what I was doing and letting me know how my responses had blessed and helped them. This is another dimension of apologetics, strengthening other believers. It is important to note an error unanswered will be accepted as the truth. Currently, the lies about God, the Bible, and Christianity are rampant and are overwhelming what little apologetics exist.

The essential point is I do not judge what I do by how many debates I win or souls I save, because the first doesn't matter and I can't do the latter in any event. My goal in my walk with God is to be a faithful servant, and I will leave the results to God, and in my calling that includes apologetics.

WHAT IS APOLOGETICS?

Apologetics in a formal sense is the study of the reasoning and evidence that supports the Christian faith. It is both focused and broad; focused in that its chief concern is Christianity. It is broad in that Christianity touches on a wide range of subjects such as philosophy, languages, linguistics, history, and science, to name just a few. Philosophy is important on several fronts; not only are there the classical arguments for the existence of God, but also the study of knowledge and how we come to know what we know, the study of logic and even the nature of truth itself. There is also the issue of moral philosophy, how we know what is good or evil, and even whether there are such things.

Christianity is a religion grounded in a book: The Bible. This involves the study of ancient languages and the issues around translations, which often gets into linguistic issues, i.e., how languages work. It also involves textual criticism or the study of the thousands of ancient manuscripts and the reliability of the text. Reflecting on John 3:16, or any other verse, how do we know John wrote these words? The whole subject of reliability and the issues surrounding reliability brings in the subjects of ancient history, archeology, and the standard tests and methods used to assess the reliability of documents.

In addition to ancient history there is also church history. What happened in the early days of the church, how did it form, how did the various books we find in the Bible come to be there and why were others excluded? This is not only restricted to the early history of the Church but includes the history of the Church down through history. Why were there Crusades, and what was the Inquisition all about?

Often these various areas intersect when it comes to particular questions such as dealing with supposed errors and contradictions in the Bible or questions of authorship as in "did the Apostle John write the Gospel of John". Finally, there is the large subject of the intersection of science and Christianity.

The importance of these various areas will rise or diminish depending on the person. For example, philosophical issues of the existence of God will likely be very important when in discussion with an atheist but will just as likely be of little importance when talking to a non-Christian theist. Going forward, I will normally contrast Christianity with atheism. This not to say atheists are the only group apologetics focus on, but rather to keep to the discussion here simple and straight forward.

The whole subject of apologetics is often attacked as illegitimate because it fixes on a conclusion before it begins the investigation. In short, its goal is to defend Christianity rather than to determine the truth and therefore apologetics is invalid. There are two main problems with this argument. The first is it assumes all who support apologetics were always Christians and this is just a way to support what they already believe. While this is undoubtedly true for some or even most, I, for one, was an atheist, and this was a significant factor in my interest in the subject. Also, although the study of apologetics did reinforce and strengthen some things I believed, it also changed and shaped others. In short, I went to where I believe the evidence took me.

The other problem with this argument is it sets up a false dichotomy, where the critic is nobly claiming to simply seek the truth, while the Christian is suppressing the truth in the attempt to justify what they believe. The simple fact is there is very little difference between what, for example, atheists do, and what Christians do. Both defend what they believe. While in some areas we do not know what to believe and therefore there might be a pure search for truth, even these searches operate within a whole range of assumptions and beliefs, acknowledged and unacknowledged that shape, constrain and limit our search.

Searching for the location of missing car keys, most people automatically eliminate and thus do not even consider the possibility that beings from an alternate reality stole them. I would argue this is a good thing, but it is not the only constraint we put on our searches. In the attempt to determine what is true, we are all limited by what we already believe to be true.

Normally, people state what they believe and defend what they believe when challenged. Even in academia, which, at least in theory, is supposed to be a pure search for truth, there are various schools of thought within most subject areas, and proponents of these write articles and books, arguing what they believe is correct. After all when was the last time you read a book where the author argued they were wrong? Why is it ok when an atheist is arguing they are right, but a Christian arguing they are right is somehow invalid?

Often the response is something to the effect the atheist is open to change, while the Christian is locked in. This is certainly not my experience. Granted, my position plays a role in this, but some of the most dogmatic people I have encountered have been atheists. Even if this were not the case, the simple fact is we are all resistant to changing our minds and this characteristic of humanity is not limited to religion but found in all areas of life.

This view is often grounded in a very narrow, stereotypical view of a Christian. Yet, Christianity encompasses a wide range of beliefs, even on things such as; what does it mean for the Bible to be inspired? Thus, when a Christian apologist reaches a particular conclusion that does not mean it was the only alternative open to them or they are locked into it.

Similar to this is the claim the atheist is looking at all the evidence both pro and con while apologetics only look at what supports them. Again, my experience was that when I studied religion at secular schools, only the secular point of view was taught, and when I studied apologetics, I studied both the secular and religious points of view. Since then, I have found in several decades of discussions, the vast majority of atheists I have talked to were only aware of the secular points of views. They had no knowledge of any scholarly viewpoints differing from secular beliefs. Some, as I document in my books, have gone so far as to deny reality and claim such scholars do not even exist. This is hardly an open-minded point of view.

Two Basic Approaches

As I mentioned earlier, Christianity is not a single thing but encompasses a wide range of differing points of view, so it should not be too surprising this extends to apologetics itself. As such, Christian apologetics is made up of two broad camps, Presuppositional and Evidential. Both schools are valid, and there is a lot of overlap between them, but there are key differences in their approach and particularly their starting point.

Presuppositional apologetics begins with the assumption that God exists, and to many, particularly the atheist, this seems circular as it assumes the conclusion. Yet, all arguments make some assumptions since they must start somewhere. The classic argument: "All men are mortal; Socrates is a man; therefore Socrates is mortal", assumes there are things called men, a condition called mortality, and a person called Socrates. It also assumes a rational form of argument, and some underlying principles such as the Law of Identity. All arguments must start someplace, and for the presuppositionalist apologist, the starting point is God. From this starting point, they begin to explore what this means and how it works itself out in the world. The basic claim is this provides a better understanding of the reality in which we live, than alternative approaches.

The other type of apologetics, Evidential, start with the person and the evidence they see around them. Based on this, they begin to ask questions, such as where did this come from, and draw conclusions. The evidentialist suggests the existence of God is a conclusion reached based on evidence, rather than a presupposition. Despite the difference in starting points, there is a broad overlap, such as questions of science or the reliability of the Bible.

Which is best, largely depends on your situation. While it is not completely ineffective, presuppositional apologetics will be more difficult when dealing with an atheist. On the other hand, when dealing with a theist, the presuppositionalist approach works quite well. Again, the focus should be on the person you are talking with and their questions and issues.

THE ROLE OF EVIDENCE,

Some questions asked concerning evidential apologetics is whether the role of evidence replaces or even precludes faith. Are faith and reason even compatible? Is looking at evidence somehow showing a lack of faith? Must one base their decisions only on faith, or only on reason?

Part of the issue is a misconception about faith and its relation to belief. While they are similar, and at times these words are used synonymously, there remains a distinction between them. Belief refers to whether or not you think something is true. Faith refers to whether or not you trust a belief, person, or thing.

Thinking something is true, and trusting it are related, but there are times when our belief and faith diverge. An example of a situation where this can happen is flying. People who intellectually believe that planes can and do fly, sometimes are very reluctant to get on one. Strictly speaking, their problem is not a lack of belief; it is a lack of faith.

You can see this is the way the letter of Hebrews defines faith.

Now faith is the assurance that what we hope for will come about and the certainty that what we cannot see exists. By faith our ancestors won approval. By faith we understand that time was

created by the word of God, so that what is seen was made from
things that are invisible. (Hebrews 11:1-3)

Faith is the "assurance," and "certainty" of what we hope for yet do not see. The word translated in the ISV, RSV, and NASB as "assurance" is the Greek word *hypóstasis (ὑπόστασις)*. Translated in the NIV as "being sure," and in the KJV as "substance," the word has caused some difficulty in translation for it can refer either to sense of assurance (guarantee, attestation), or it can refer to the nature (substance, essence, foundation) of something. The context here would indicate the former, faith is the assurance we have that what we hope for will happen. The word translated "certainty" (*elenchos - ἔλεγχος*) is easier to translate. It refers to verification, evidence, or proof of something, and was used in first-century writings when referring to legal proof.

Faith is the confidence in a position that goes beyond what we can fully support. Implied in this definition, and more clearly stated elsewhere in the Bible (e.g., James 2:26) is that faith is the confidence that leads us to act on our beliefs. This part of faith is seen in a little child who stands on the edge of a pool waiting to jump into the arms of their parent. The child may believe their parent will catch them, but such a belief does not always lead to them jump. It is when their belief is combined with confidence to the point that actions result (i.e., they jump into their parent's arms) that we can say they had faith.

Having defined what is meant by faith, the author then goes on to illustrate this definition with a series of examples to flesh out the definition. The combination of belief and confidence that leads to action is the hallmark of the examples that fill the rest of the chapter. By faith Abel offered a better sacrifice (v 4), Noah built the ark (v 7), Abraham left his homeland (v 8), and Moses led the Jews out of Egypt (v 29). All the examples the author gives are of people who, because of their faith, did something. As such, we end up with a definition of faith as the confidence we have in a position going beyond what the evidence supports; it is a confidence that leads to action.

That reason can serve as a basis for faith is seen in the account in Hebrews of Abraham being told to sacrifice Isaac. Hebrews tells us "Abraham was certain that God could raise the dead" (Heb 11:19). The word translated by the ISV as "certain" is the Greek word *logisamenos (λογισάμενος)*, and it means to think in a logical fashion that considers all the evidence. So, in this chapter that has been called the Hall of Faith, we have Abraham trusting God as a result of his reasoning.

Both in the Old and New Testaments, we are told to look at the evidence. Deuteronomy 13:1-3, tells us to look at the evidence to determine whether a person who claimed to be a prophet was from God or a false prophet. In 1 Corinthians 15, Paul gives a reasoned defense of the Resurrection, challenging those in Corinth who doubted his claim to check it out for themselves.

When some Jews gathered around Jesus in the temple determined to see if He was the Messiah, He replied, "I have told you, but you don't believe it. The actions that I do in my Father's name testify on my behalf" (John 10:25). In answering their question Jesus appealed not to a statement of faith, but the evidence, the things he did, to demonstrated who he truly was. He did not just expect them to believe his claims. In fact, in John 5:31 Jesus said that "If I testify on my own behalf, my testimony is not trustworthy." This is not a statement his testimony is not trustworthy, but rather the true Messiah would come with supporting evidence. Jesus then proceeded to cite the testimony of John the Baptist (John 5:33-35), the works of the Father (e.g., miracles) He has done (5:36), and the statements in the Scriptures about Him (5:37-40) as evidence of who He was.

There is nothing incompatible with evidence and reason, on the one hand, and faith on the other. Paul tells us to "test everything. Hold on to what is good" (1 Thessalonians 5:21). How are we to do this without using evidence and reason? Nowhere do we

7

see a call to a blind faith cut off from evidence and reason. Instead, we are pointed to the evidence. This is why the Jews were called to remember the Exodus and what God had done, and Christians the resurrection, for these were things only the true God could do.

As the Jewish leaders challenged Jesus and were about to stone Him for claiming to be God, he did not tell them to have blind faith but instead pointed them to the evidence of who he was,

> *"If I'm not doing my Father's actions, don't believe me. But if I'm doing them, even though you don't believe me, believe the actions, so that you may know and understand that the Father is in me and I am in the Father". (John 10:37-38)*

DOING APOLOGETICS BADLY

While we are called to defend the faith, that is not a blank check to do whatever we want. As we saw above, the command to defend our faith in 1 Peter 3:15-16 starts with a call to defend, immediately followed by a caution on how to do this, and by inference how not to do this,

> *Instead, exalt the Messiah as Lord in your lives. Always be prepared to give a defense to everyone who asks you to explain the hope you have. But do this gently and respectfully, keeping a clear conscience, so that those who speak evil of your good conduct in the Messiah will be ashamed of slandering you.*

As a fairly new Christian attending a secular college, I saw a group of traveling Christians come to the college one week and began preaching next to the bell tower in the center of the campus. Initially, I thought this was a good thing, preaching the Gospel to those who needed to hear it. However, as I watched them over the week, it quickly became clear their message was the opposite of the "gently and respectfully" called for in 1 Peter.

Their style was purposefully to antagonize, aimed at creating a confrontation. They would call the students immoral, using derogatory names simply for walking by, and then when challenged would respond with fire and brimstone type responses. Thus, over the week there were a lot of heat generated but little light. Toward the end of the week, the students lost interest in them, and the crowds diminished. This attitude among the students would in a few decades by codified into the Internet rule, 'Don't feed the trolls.' The students learned quickly there was nothing to be gained in talking to these people, and doing so would only get them insulted and aggravated. Thus, the best thing was to avoid them and not respond. The crowds diminishing, they left at the end of the week heading to the next campus.

Before they left, I went up to one of them and asked what they hoped to accomplish. They saw themselves as proclaiming the truth, defending the faith, and calling the lost to repentance. They used the tactics they did because it attracted attention. These were lofty and noble goals, but I do not believe the tactics they used gave them the results they wanted. I believe the result was much more the opposite, for they reinforced the negative stereotype of Christians often seen in the media. I believe many people that week had their walls reinforced and strengthen, not brought down.

More problematic, is that these preachers not only taught the students Christianity was a religion of hate and anger, but worse, it was best not to talk to Christians at all, at least about religion for nothing good would come of it. Thus, not only did they drive these people away from God, but they helped build a wall, making it much harder for them ever to come back.

As a Christian Apologist, far too much of my time is focused on addressing why Christians do not always act like Christians. This, of course, involves the big issues in history, such as the Inquisition and the Crusades, but it also includes questions about groups such as the Westboro Baptist Church and even questions that begin, "I knew a Christian who..."

The internet and modern culture have only exacerbated this problem. With all of its positives, the internet has coarsened the culture. Before, when you wanted to insult someone you normally had to do it to their face, or at least in a way that was traceable back to you. You had to own your insult. The internet and its cryptic names that allow people to remain anonymous has revealed the darkness that is in the human heart.

This is compounded by a culture where it is much easier to get noticed by breaking the norms than following them. Being somehow provocative is a much easier road to success than being serious, and there is a temptation here. Think of all the books purporting to be about a Hollywood Star, Washington politician, etc., that makes all the talk shows and news programs because of one or two sensational claims.

The problem is that fame, or in the case of the campus preachers, crowds, are fleeting. They do not matter. What matters is the results. Are people getting saved? Are lives being transformed? Of course, the campus preachers might respond, 'how can we transform lives if no one listens to us? We need to attract the crowd first.' Thus, the trap.

We are called to proclaim and defend the faith. We are not called to attract large crowds or even to get results. The results of our work are in God's hands, not ours. We have the great privilege to be part of the process of saving people and transforming lives, but that does not mean we will always see the results. People in the military tend to move around a lot and as a result, the vast majority of the Christians who were critical in the process of my salvation were not in a position to know about my conversion. If they remember me at all, it will be as the atheist with which they once argued. Yet they were faithful to God's calling, and He was able to use them in the process of my conversion.

Ultimately, unless you keep the fact you are a Christian secret, at which point you have a different problem, the simple truth is that we all live 1 Peter 3:15 every day, we are all testifying about our faith. The only real question is do we do it badly or do it well. Are we closer to the campus preachers driving people from God, or are we following the pattern of 1 Peter 3:16, bringing down the walls that people build to keep God away?

DOING APOLOGETICS WELL

How does one do apologetics well? To start with, one must know what it is they are defending. 1 Peter 3:15 says we should "Always be prepared to give a defense to everyone who asks you to explain the hope you have." Why do you have hope? Why are you a Christian? This is not asking why you attend the church you do, but why do you have a relationship with Jesus at all? Nor is this asking for a recitation of the theology behind the plan of salvation. It is asking about you, your life, and why do YOU have the hope you have. If you do not have an answer for this question, you need to spend time in prayer until you do.

GROUNDED IN TRUTH

It is also important to remember you are defending the truth. In John 14:6 Jesus said he was, "the way, the truth, and the life." Have you ever thought about why those three? Of all the things he could have said, he chose those three. The way is pretty clear, as he follows this by "No one comes to the Father except through me." Jesus is the only way to God. Life is also pretty easy to understand. The goal of salvation is eternal life, and that is found in Jesus.

Why pick truth? Why not mercy, or compassion? In 1 John it says, "God is Love" (1 John 4:8), so why not "I am the way, the love, and the life?" Certainly, Jesus could have said this, and it would have been correct. However, he chose to say "the truth" instead. Truth is very important, since earlier in the Gospel we are

11

told "God is spirit, and those who worship him must worship in spirit and truth" (John 4:24).

In defending our faith, we must ground ourselves in the truth. Very early in my Christian walk, a Sunday School teacher came over to my house and was sharing how NASA scientists had found a day missing in their calculations. This missing day, he said, corresponded to the time in Joshua where the sun stood still (Joshua 10:12-13), and the time God caused the Sun's shadow to move back ten steps (in 2 Kings 20:8-11) which together make up a full day. He was a little disappointed when I explained to him it was impossible for NASA to have found a day missing but he seemed to accept it. Regardless, on Sunday he told the story in his Sunday school class. I asked him about it and he replied it was just too good not to use.

Lies and errors can not defend the truth. Any short-term gains will be short-lived, and the damage done will be long-lasting. The ends (defending what you believe to be true) do not justify the means (using what you know to be false). This is not always as easy as it may at first seem, because often we not only lie to others to defend the truth, we lie to ourselves.

Nowhere is this more apparent than when it comes to the church. A significant part of my work as an apologist is answering questions about why Christians do not always act like Christians. Granted, it would be much easier if I could say, "They were not Christians. Real Christians would not do such things." As much as I might wish to make such a claim, I cannot.

The truth is, Christians have done some pretty awful things down through history, nor should we be surprised by this. After all, a core teaching of Christianity is "all have sinned and continue to fall short of God's glory" (Romans 3:23). We are not saved because we are better people or sin less than others, "For by such grace you have been saved through faith. This does not come from you; it is the gift of God and not the result of actions, to put a stop to all boasting" (Ephesians 2:8-9). As Christians, we have not ceased to

sin, for as the Apostle John says, "If we say that we do not have any sin, we are deceiving ourselves and we're not being truthful to ourselves" (1 John 1:8). On what basis can we say things like the Inquisition, could not have been done by Christians?

Frankly, such denials in the end are not even effective as the argument breaks down into special pleading where Christians who do things we like are "real Christians," and those who do things we disapprove of are not real Christians. The truth may not always be easy, but the truth is always a better defense.

How do I answer arguments like the Inquisition? First, I start with the truth, however uncomfortable, there were certainly things done that were evil, and I acknowledge it. I also put it into context. The Inquisition came, not from the early church or the teachings of Jesus. What we commonly think of as the Inquisition was, as a matter of history, an aberration in the teaching of the church. Both before and after the maximum penalty of the church was excommunication. Even at the time of the Inquisition, it was not universally practiced by all Christians.

Where did the Inquisition originate? It emerged from the confluence of two historical factors, first was the rise of anti-clericalism in the 12th century that began to put pressure on the church. This coincided with the second factor: a revival of Roman Law as a better approach to governing. One aspect of Roman Law was when there were questions about heresy, a judge could make an *inquisiti* to investigate the matter. While Roman Law permitted torture, at first it was not used, though this too changed over time.

Thus, the Inquisition was evil, but it was not Christians carrying out the teachings of Jesus, or the Bible. It was Christians caught up in the historical trends of their day. It should not be minimized or ignored, but serve as a warning. The warning is not the warning the critic would have us believe, that we should reject Christianity or even religion as a whole. There is nothing inherently religious with groups being pressured by their opposition, or groups being caught up in the historical trends of their day. Such things are found in all types of groups throughout history. The real lesson here is for Christians to be careful how they think and react to those who disagree, something Jesus and the Bible are clear about. They should also be careful about being caught up in the trends of the day. This is a more difficult answer, but I think it is a better one.

PRIORITIZING PEOPLE

It is also important to keep the end goal in mind when doing apologetics and the goal is to minister to people. At the end of the Gospel of John, Jesus asked Peter three times, "Do you love me." Three times Peter said that he did. Some see significance in the interchangeability of the words used for "love" (*agapaó / phileó - ἀγαπάω / φιλέω*), but it is hard to find support for this distinction in the first-century usage of these terms, as they were often used synonymously.

Rather than trying to get him to focus on a particular type of love, Jesus asked three times, because Peter had denied Jesus three times. The point here is not the type of love we have, but what we do with it, for each time Jesus responses, "Feed my sheep." This is the Triangle of Divine Love. God first loves us. We love God, and we show our love for God by ministering to others.

This love should be at the heart of all we do, including apologetics. This may at first seem very strange for some, after all, why study ancient languages, archeology, philosophy, science or any of the other myriad of subjects if the goal is to love others? Yet, think of all the detailed subjects like chemistry and microbiology a physician needs to study to effectively help people.

One can do all this for the wrong reasons. If you study apologetics to be the best debater, one who can always defeat their opponent, then you are serving yourself not God. In every encounter, every discussion, every debate you should always ask who is the audience, and what is the goal?

In discussions with another person, the audience is the other person, and there really would not be an opponent in the strict sense of the word. However, when in a group this question can become very complicated very quickly. People are individuals and must be treated as such. For example, say I am in a discussion with an atheist and another Christian, should my responses be aimed at 1) Breaking down the walls of the atheist? 2) Building up the faith of the other Christian? Granted, I would like to do both, but let's say as the discussion develops, I need to focus on one at the expense of the other, as is very likely to happen.

The simple fact is there is no easy answer to that question, because no one is just "an atheist" and likewise no one is just "a Christian." If the atheist was a hardcore neo-atheist, with a long history of attacking and trying to destroy the faith of others, while the Christian was a new Christian who was unfamiliar with the history and evidence backing up the Christian faith, I might very well focus on building up the faith of the Christian. In this case, the opponent would be the atheist, and the audience would be the Christian.

On the other hand, if the Christian fit the negative stereotype of an apologist, one whose main goal is the defeat of anyone who disagrees, while the atheist was a person with honest questions, it is very possible I would change my focus and my opponent would be the other Christian, and the audience would be atheist.

Never is the situation even as clear cut as this, for unlike the exchanges of sound bites and slogans that today routinely masquerade as discussion, real discussions are very complex things. Even when limited to two people, there are a lot of factors, often in conflict with each other and dynamically changing. A discussion that starts on the question of the reliability of the Bible, can suddenly swerve into any number of different rabbit holes and before you know it you are discussing the Thirty years war in Europe or something else seemingly unrelated. As a result, who is the opponent and who is the audience could change from moment to moment.

The key is to focus on the individuals, over the arguments. Even when in a discussion with multiple people, and someone for the moment falls into the role of an opponent, they do not cease to be first and foremost a person. This is one of the reasons it is so important to remain grounded in the truth. In the dynamics of a discussion, there are at times debaters' tricks that could be quite effective when it comes to "winning the debate" and while they may or may not be quite dishonest, they are not grounded in the truth.

For example, many issues are very complex and often it is possible to summarize them in a negative way that is not an accurate reflection of the person's position but does make the position easy to dismiss. You create a straw man, label it the position you are opposing, and then proceed to knock it down. One does not have to watch very many public debates, to see this trick employed. It is not something an apologist should do, for it puts the position ahead of the person, and is not grounded in truth.

BEING A LISTENER

It can be very difficult to know what to do at any given moment with all the complexities involved in prioritizing people and all the dynamics within a discussion. The only way you will have any hope of doing this is to become a listener first. Again, this builds off the other two, for to accurately and truthfully respond to an individual, you must know who they are as an individual and what they believe, and that requires listening.

Listening is important because in one sense there are no atheists, Buddhist, or Christians there are only individuals, each one unique in their own way, each one different from the other. As C. S. Lewis put it,

> There are no ordinary people. You have never talked to a mere mortal. Nations, cultures, arts, civilizations—these are mortal, and their life is to ours as the life of a gnat. But it is immortals

whom we joke with, work with, marry, snub, and exploit—im-
mortal horrors or everlasting splendors.

Everyone we meet is a unique individual, and no two are alike. There is a danger in apologetics to forget this, and see someone as a label, not a person; to see them as a puzzle to be solved rather than a person. In some sense this is understandable, if someone spends a lot of time studying a group like atheists, then there will be a tendency to believe the next atheist you meet lines up with what you have studied, but they often won't.

Some atheists see religion as a sort of necessary delusion, something needed by society to make people better, but without any actual basis in fact. Other atheists see religion as a dangerous delusion, something that makes people bad, and something to eliminate. These are widely different points of view.

There are also atheists whose rejection of God is grounded in a supposed lack of evidence. There are others whose reasons are grounded in a bad experience with a person or church, and still others who dislike the restrictions that a belief in God implies, and yet others who drifted into atheism without any serious consideration. Combine these four reasons with the two types, and you already have eight different types of atheists. Yet there are many more types and many more reasons and if that was not enough there many more factors. In short, every atheist is unique with their own beliefs and reasons for holding them. They are people and not just a label.

This is not a problem unique to apologetics, as we see it in every endeavor of human life. It is a necessary evil that is built into language, and into our ability to think and reason. Some call for the elimination of all labels, but this simply is not possible. Every word is a label, so to reject all labels is to reject communication. The solution is not to reject labels, but to remember they are labels, and those with whom we talk are not, they are unique individuals.

Thus, rather than assume the person before us matches some label, we must listen. Rather than launching into our canned speech for atheists as soon as we find out a person does not believe in God, we need to listen to what they believe and think, which will take time. People are complex and so are their beliefs. Their thoughts on God are often very personal. In our current culture, we are not supposed to talk about politics and religion, which makes it even more difficult to discuss. People build walls for a reason, and they protect them.

When having a conversation with a person who feels comfortable enough to talk about spiritual matters with you, the initial reasons they give will probably not be the core issues. It is not that they are dishonest; rather again people have many reasons for their beliefs and the first ones they share are not likely to be the ones that goes to the heart of the matter.

Based on the discussions in which I have been involved, it can often take quite some time and many conversations before you begin to get to what are the core issues, and these are often significantly different from where the discussion originally started. A discussion can easily start with questions about the reliability of the Bible, and end with issues of anger with God.

So perhaps one of the most important skills in apologetics is listening. This must be done in light of the first two; it must prioritize people and be grounded in truth; in short, it must be built on a relationship with a real interest in the person. It cannot simply be a means to an end, nor should the relationship be focused only on spiritual matters. People should be treated as whole individuals. For me, this is one of the more enjoyable parts and the heart of the matter because people are interesting.

AVOID AGENDAS

Another problem with doing apologetics is that as Christians we have many beliefs which are important to us, but are not critical for someone beginning a relationship with God. For example, I believe in the Inerrancy of Scripture, but I do not believe this is a requirement for salvation because after all, not all Christians share this belief. Some who reject inerrancy have a very strong view of the reliability of Scripture. They trust the scripture, and in fact may not be able to point to anything that is in error, but are just not willing to say it must be without error. Some see Scripture as more the product of men guided by God, but not free from errors. While still others say that if you cannot completely trust every word, then you cannot trust anything it says. In short, there is a wide range of views among Christians on the reliability of Scripture.

Talking with non-believers, it is very common for this issue to come up at some point and that immediately raises the question of which view to defend. The easiest answer would be to defend your own view, after all, that is the one you know the best, but therein lies the problem, for your view depends on you. Let's say, like me, you believe in inerrancy and the person you are talking to had not thought much about this issue. As you explain your belief in inerrancy, let's further say the person finds this belief very difficult to accept. After all, not even all Christians accept it and if you insist on this view, the result will be rather than removing a brick from their wall, you have added a brick to their wall, a brick labeled inerrancy.

This is why I normally do not talk about inerrancy with non-Christians, except to point out it is not a required belief. For those who claim a single error in the Bible means we cannot trust it, this would be very disturbing. Yet, this argument is simply wrong, and more importantly, it is irrelevant.

In any communication, there are many steps, but they can be summarized as the sender, the sending mechanism, the transmission, the receiving mechanism, and the receiver. As you talk to someone on your cell phone, there is you, your phone, the cellar network system, their cell phone, and finally the person with whom you are talking. Problems at any step can result in problems communicating.

With most people's view of the Bible, you have God, the prophet, the textual transmission, the translation, and person. Inerrancy holds the first two steps, God and the prophet, resulted in no errors. I also believe the next two steps, textual transmission, and translation, are very reliable. This leaves us to read and understand, and that is where I believe virtually all of the errors occur.

I am very willing to say, and believe, that what the prophets wrote by inspiration of God is inerrant. I am not willing to say my understanding of what they wrote is inerrant. Rather, I am pretty sure it is flawed in some places and that is why I continue to study and strive to do better. If the slightest flaw in our knowledge renders our entire understanding worthless then none of us could ever hope to know anything.

I do not argue for my personal belief of inerrancy when this issue does come up, instead I argue for reliability. There is a very practical reason for this as well. Inerrancy is virtually impossible to demonstrate without getting into theological arguments such as the nature of God. There are simply too many places were to do not have enough historical information to say, one way or the other, whether the biblical account is accurate. For example, we know when Joseph was sold into slavery, the price was correct for the likely period he lived, but we do not have a bill of sale and thus cannot say no error was made recording the price. This may seem trivial and in many ways it is, but it is why some Christians believe the Bible and yet do not see a need to accept inerrancy.

On the other hand, reliability is far easier to demonstrate. In the example above, the sales price does conform to the period, which is very significant given that critics claim the story was written hundreds of years later when such details would have been unknown. Relevant to Christians, the key teaching of the Bible is the life, death, and resurrection of Jesus, for which the evidence is very strong that the Bible is reliable.

The important point here is not inerrancy vs. reliability, but the questions or issues of the person and your beliefs. You may believe that the Genesis' day was a literal 24-hour day and the earth is only ten thousand years old. If the person you are talking to sees no problem with Genesis' account and it is not an issue for them, you should not raise it regardless of their view of the age of the earth. Likewise, maybe their understanding of Church history is different from yours, but again if it is not something that keeps them from God why focus on it?

This again builds on the early principles of prioritizing people and listening to them, to learn their issues, questions, and problems. It also needs to be grounded in truth and we should not gloss over problems but recognize that among Christians there are differences of opinion in certain areas. The goal is to bring people into a relationship with God, not to get them to agree with us.

There is one other factor here that can help guide us, which is the role of the third commandment. Many see the third commandment, "You are not to misuse the name of the LORD your God, because the LORD will not leave the one who misuses his name unpunished," as basically a command against swearing, but the command is much broader. A much greater problem is using God's name to bolster your own beliefs and positions, pushing your agenda, as if it were God's agenda.

A clear example of this would be if a politician claims God would support their bill, but this can also happen with Christians talking about the Bible. Saying I believe a particular teaching or I think the Bible teaches it is fine, but the closer I get to saying that disagreeing with me is disagreeing with God on that teaching, however it is couched, the more I risk running afoul of the third commandment. Speaking about things upon which all Christians agree is pretty safe, but when you get into areas of disagreement among Christians, we must not assume ours is the only valid position, however much we may think we are right.

One way I think about this is there are pre-conversion issues and post-conversion issues. Reflecting about your own conversion experience, think about how much you have learned since your conversion. I will talk about whatever is a particular issue for the person that is keeping them from God, but ultimately there is only one real pre-conversion issue needing to be dealt with, their relationship with God.

DEPEND ON THE BODY

Some people are reluctant to engage in certain conversations, because they are afraid they will get a question they cannot answer, or even worse, they will confront an argument that will challenge their own faith. As for having your faith challenged it is understandable why people think this way. Modern Western culture is a secular culture based on science and reason, at least in its self-serving assessment of itself. It is a culture which has long since moved beyond being neutral and into a dismissiveness increasingly tinged with hostility toward Christianity.

Thus, it is not unusual to see stories or shows with scholars questioning the reliability of the Bible or the existence of God. Those supportive of traditional religious views are often put in the same category as UFOs and conspiracy theories. Combined with an overall decline in biblical literacy among Christians and the trend to see Sunday school as primarily for the young, today the average Christians is largely unequipped to handle even the most basic questions people have.

The common view among non-Christians is the Bible is an ancient book having little if anything to say to the modern world and religion itself is a destructive force. The faster we put it behind us, the better. Consider the often-cited claim that religion is the cause of most wars. Religion has caused very few wars, rather base human flaws like greed, desire for land, power, glory, etc., are behind most wars. Even the wars where religion was a major factor, such as the Crusades and the Thirty Years War in Europe, have many other factors than religion. In fact, in the Thirty Years War, the religious issue was settled with a treaty halfway through, yet the war continued, with the latter half being the worst part of the war.

It is hard to fight the culture, particularly when so much of the Church, at least in the West, is in retreat, with Europe clearly in a post-Christian phase and America not far behind. Biblical literacy is on the decline, not just within the broader culture, but within the church as well. It is ironic that this decline is occurring at the same time the resources and tools for serious study have never been more available and easily accessible. The need is growing, the ease and ability are growing, and yet Biblical literacy is reaching record lows.

Add to this the prevalence of topical sermons on Sunday morning, sermons preaching on a topic the pastor has chosen rather than teaching through a book. Even when a pastor has a series on a book, the actual preaching is still at times basically topical. Consider the following comments,

> Some of the details are fuzzy for me but I will probably never forget one Sunday morning being at church when during the sermon it was said that the church was finishing its series through the book of Matthew. My friend and I turned and looked at each other with the same thought, "I did not know the sermon series was working through Matthew the past few weeks." We were completely confused. (Topical vs. Expository vs. The Underlying Issue, 2016)

While this is not a problem at my current church, we have all been there. The Pastor announces they will be preaching from a particular passage, but at the end of the sermon, you realize the passage was merely a launching point for a topic message. This is not an indictment of all topical sermons. There is a need for them, and they are useful, but they are dangerous as well, for stringing together a series of verses to teach a message rarely allows one to understand the context and meaning of each verse. A good pastor will respect the context of each verse chosen, but you run a much greater risk of getting the preachers message rather than the Biblical message, and such sermons are not very good at building Biblical literacy by themselves.

A key aspect of defending the faith is a knowledge of what it is you are defending. Someone asks you for a reason for the hope you have, you should, at a minimum, know what hope you have. What is it you believe? Why are you a Christian? Why are you not some other religion? Why are you not an atheist?

This does not mean every Christian should be a trained apologist, ready to answer every conceivable question. The New Testament makes clear, there are many parts of the body of Christ. While we are all called to minister to others, we are each called to specialize in different areas, if you are not called to be an apologist that is fine, others will be.

You will get questions for which you do not have an answer and that is fine. One of my favorite responses is, 'That is a good question, and I do not know the answer. Let me find out and I will get back to you.' I like this answer, because it can become the basis for a discussion and thus a relationship. Of course, if you include the last part, now you must go and find an answer. A great place to start is with your Church. While you may not have an answer, chances are very good someone in your Church will, if you do not know where to begin, start with your Sunday school teacher or the pastor or priest. They will be able to point you in the right direction, if they do not have the answer.

LEAVING THE HEAVY LIFTING TO GOD

Will you see results, if you are grounded in the truth, prioritizing people, being a listener, avoiding agendas, and depending on the Body of Christ? Occasionally, but not often. Apologetics is important work, but rarely sees tangible results in the way a pastor or evangelist will. When you look at a very tall building you may ponder how tall it is, but how often do you think about the foundation upon which it rests?

The work of apologetics is foundational in nature and often goes unnoticed. As you remove the bricks in the walls that people have built up to protect themselves from God, often you will not even know you have made progress. As I said earlier, many of the most effective Christians I met with never saw the impact they had on my life. They planted seeds, seeds they may very well have thought were planted on barren ground, and in many respects that was true, but they planted seeds that later the Holy Spirit would use to bring life.

This is the true work of apologetics. It is not winning arguments, which is meaningless. It is the not work of an evangelist, who is there at the harvest. It is the planting of seeds that can be used by the Holy Spirit to soften the heart. This, in and of itself, requires faith and requires us to trust God for the rest of the process. Unlike the pastor, evangelist, or teacher, the results of an apologist are often known only to God. Yet, it remains a work that at least to some extent, we are all called to do.

> *Instead, exalt the Messiah as Lord in your lives. Always be prepared to give a defense to everyone who asks you to explain the hope you have. But do this gently and respectfully, keeping a clear conscience, so that those who speak evil of your good conduct in the Messiah will be ashamed of slandering you. (1 Peter 3:15)*

TOPICAL LINE DRIVES

Straight to the Point in under 44 Pages

All Topical Line Drives volumes are priced at $4.99 print and 99¢ in all ebook formats.

Available

(The titles of planned volumes may change before release.)

Generous Quantity Discounts Available
Dealer Inquiries Welcome
Energion Publications — P.O. Box 841
Gonzalez, FL 32560
Website: http://energionpubs.com
Phone: (850) 525-3916

ALSO FROM ENERGION PUBLICATIONS

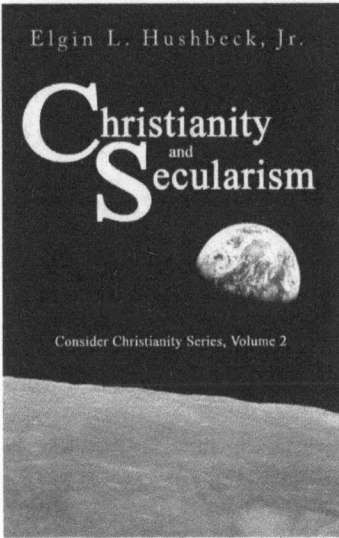

Elgin L. Hushbeck, Jr.

Christianity
and
Secularism

Consider Christianity Series, Volume 2

Hushbeck is truly a present day champion in defense of Christianity and the Bible.

Dr. Robert McKibben
United Methodist Pastor,
Retired

BY ELGIN HUSHBECK, JR.

Closely argued, deeply informed, highly sensitive to the issues.

Dallas Willard
Philosopher and author

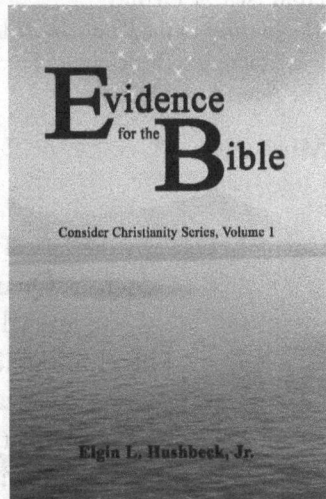

Evidence
for the **B**ible

Consider Christianity Series, Volume 1

Elgin L. Hushbeck, Jr.

MORE FROM ENERGION PUBLICATIONS

Personal Study

Holy Smoke! Unholy Fire	Bob McKibben	$14.99
The Jesus Paradigm	David Alan Black	$17.99
When People Speak for God	Henry Neufeld	$17.99
The Sacred Journey	Chris Surber	$11.99

Christian Living

Faith in the Public Square	Robert D. Cornwall	$16.99
Grief: Finding the Candle of Light	Jody Neufeld	$8.99
Crossing the Street	Robert LaRochelle	$16.99
Life in the Spirit	J. Hamilton Weston	$12.99

Bible Study

Learning and Living Scripture	Lentz/Neufeld	$12.99
Inspiration: Hard Questions, Honest Answers	Alden Thompson	$29.99
Colossians & Philemon	Allan R. Bevere	$12.99
Ephesians: A Participatory Study Guide	Robert D. Cornwall	$9.99

Theology

Christian Archy	David Alan Black	$9.99
The Politics of Witness	Allan R. Bevere	$9.99
Ultimate Allegiance	Robert D. Cornwall	$9.99
From Here to Eternity	Bruce Epperly	$5.99
The Journey to the Undiscovered Country	William Powell Tuck	$9.99
Eschatology: A Participatory Study Guide	Edward W. H. Vick	$9.99
The Adventist's Dilemma	Edward W. H. Vick	$14.99

Ministry

Clergy Table Talk	Kent Ira Groff	$9.99
Thrive	Ruth Fletcher	$14.99
Out of the Office: A Theology of Ministry	Bob Cornwall	$9.99

Generous Quantity Discounts Available

Dealer Inquiries Welcome

Energion Publications — P.O. Box 841

Gonzalez, FL_ 32560

Website: http://energionpubs.com

Phone: (850) 525-3916

www.ingramcontent.com/pod-product-compliance
Lightning Source LLC
Chambersburg PA
CBHW011750020426
42331CB00014B/3346